The Music Behind Me

poems by

Felice Aull

ISBN-13:978-0615700670

Alabaster Leaves Publishing
1840 West 220th Street, Suite 300
Torrance, California 90501

Dedication

For my dear family, living and dead

Acknowledgments

I thank the editors of the following publications where these poems or their earlier versions first appeared: *Ekphrasis*: "Alice Neel Paints a Portrait"; *Facets*: "Prison Escape," "Gramercy Park"; *The Healing Muse*: "A Small Thing"; *Margie Reiew/The American Journal of Poetry*: "Ghost Bar"; *The Mom Egg*: "Daughter in Her Eighth Month"; *Poet Lore*: "Camp Counselors Make Out"; *Third Wednesday*: "Sky Watch," "Stunning Blows"; *Umbrella*: "Forget That"; *The Write Place At the Write Time*: "The Lure," "Remnants of Sound."

Contents

Prison Escape

In prison are men who
write poems, word song
that flutters against the walls
seeking space to float
over the wire fences. Outside,

do people feel the air move?
Butterfly beats arising from
some unmarked enclave, whispers
that breathe soft on the cheek.

Ghost Bar

I keep expecting the bar to close,
the worn building used up
like the occasional men
who hover outside it
stubble on their sunken faces
worn cigarette stalks
gripped between their gums.
Are they pausing between drinks
or waiting for an invitation?
It's a corner bar you can't see into,
one outside wall covered in posters
that are mysteriously exchanged
new for old, latest for passé.
Someone must make money
from the rental for that wall—
probably not the bartender though
if there is a bartender.
Music never splashes out
onto the sidewalk because the door
rarely opens and when it does,
slightly, there's still no music
only brown must and the ghost
of past St. Patrick's Days
when that bar exploded
with bagpipe players wearing kilts
sounding their drones and marching
into the startled street.

Gramercy Park

is where, when you are inside
you don't look out
and where, from outside
you look in through gaps
between black bars
whose presence preserves
the inside so that outsiders
will admire what's there
and where, from the twilight zone
of homelessness,
you sit at the park perimeter
and look at nothing.

I love the strong, tall trees,
the graceful willows,
the blazing azaleas
in their time. I am restored
by these, grateful
to walk and turn each corner.
There was a day in June though
that broke my stride.
Inside,

a wedding party posing.
In white, the pale bride
shyly smiling, in black
the others sleek and slim.
The park was green, green,
ripe with health. Outside
walkers gasped, stared,
could barely move on.
When we did, there he was,
his undershirt gray,
his face slumped inside himself.

My donations are made by check,
they're tax deductible, but
the third time around
it was all too much.
He took my dollar, rising
to thank me, "Dear,"
yet even so, I couldn't
pass him, or the trees,
or the bride any more.

The Man on a Box

He lives on a milk crate
beneath the steam vent
where the dry cleaner
finds him
each morning
next door to
the grocery store—
does someone
provide the snack bag
he eats from
It's small
He's small
self-contained
with the crate
he must have carried
in the rain
to the side street
where an awning
is cover
just for him
He doesn't beg
and doesn't speak
to passersby
or to himself
I saw him walking once
some blocks away
He was exploring
the possibilities.

The Music behind Me

on the city street where I walked
was loud, bounced and flung
me around so even though
I was annoyed at the sound
that made me turn,
I felt giddy. I'm glad

I didn't frown but
he wasn't looking
in my direction. He was
steering his wheelchair
like a ship through the waves
of walkers, the radio
a mast head, the tiny
Stars & Stripes pronouncing
his right to the seas. Now

we skipped and bopped to
the beat of his baton, to
the tunes that carried us,
cruise ship passengers
sailing Second Avenue,
sailing together 'til
he disembarked.

Systems of Transit

Subway zither music
The Third Man

I do not remember my birth
or the ocean swells
that heaved us
to a new country
but the zither reminds me
of what I don't remember

Potent soundtrack
The Third Man
He was Orson Welles
evil and charming
pursued in the sewers
of postwar Vienna
At his funeral (the real one)
his lover (Alida Vali)
walked toward us slowly
stonefaced, on a long road
then passed,
moving out of the frame.
She never looked back

but I am back imagining
our flight from Vienna,
the tangled route
through Europe, me
in diapers stuffed with money
We hid like *The Third Man*
appearing, disappearing

Now a new millennium,
this subterranean system,
this zither strummed

by a silent Asian man
No need for him to sing,
to stumble in a foreign tongue—

his music sings
and I wonder about him
playing "Darling Clementine"
a song of the frontier
the American West—
he could be Korean
Vietnamese
native-and-fluently-American

simply a musician

Notes from an Alpine Vacation

Enveloped in a cloud of quilt,
cozy in my European bed,
I am reading a novel
written in English
by an Italian woman who
lives half her life in Kenya.
German, my first language,
is spoken here in South Tyrol
where Austria trumps Italy,
though this is Italy.
I stumble through it,
speaking with Frau innkeeper
who's bilingual, but not in English.
In Kenya in the novel,
displaced white women
live edgily, not sure if they enjoy it.

The Alps in April are green, the valleys mild.
Forty miles south, the town
where years ago we hid, mother and baby
in transit through dark times.
We spoke the languages hoping
to pass (mother speaking, hoping,
baby clinging). Now my own child
lives a global life in Kenya.
Swahili, safari, malaria,
jacaranda, wildebeest, drought—
she learns the language.

In South Tyrol the apple trees
flaunt pink-white blossoms
symmetrically along the hillsides
and I'm afraid
of losing the language.

International Public Health Worker

You bring me earrings,
a small silver box,
blue stones mined by
dark people I will never know.
This is your way of
staying bound to me,
the cord stretching from
continent to continent,
my fear, your daring,
the arc suspended
now taut, now slack.

Journey of the Tibetan Belt

For three months I've been afraid.

A belt of cloth, red,
tiny stitches like beads
sewn by fingers long dead.
Brought to us from Tibet
by our traveling daughter
who'd been sent there
to do her work.
She'd chosen it carefully
while breathing carefully
that spare atmosphere.

Musty and shop-worn,
Needs to be cleaned she had said.
Three months in the closet 'til I dared.

Referred from one cleaner
to the next to
Ask for Eddie who worries
the cloth is too fragile,
sending me downtown
to short old buildings
where vaudeville once played,
and to George—a cleaner for 40 years.
George is consulted—
mysteriously—where is he?
by the Filipino clerk
who in minutes assures me
no problem and
exchanges this cloth
once worn by dark- haired women

with cracked skin and thick blood,
for a bland printout
one belt—black red cotton beaded.
I leave, holding my sea level breath,
daughter now packing for Africa.

Daughter in Her Eighth Month

Approaching the predicted
midpoint of her life
she is now profoundly pregnant.
It is her first, and no technology
was needed, only the hormones
released by love, and a watchful womb.
Grandmotherhood approaches,
a state I did not crave, just as
I did not crave to be a mother
until she thumped her way
into my world, as now her fetal girl—
that floating fingered shadow
the ultrasound detects,
detecting lack which means
she'll have a daughter too—
is pummeling her.
That's how our babes enlist us.
I feel the tiny fingers pull me
into, through, blood on blood,
we three are sliding, slipping toward
the edge of separation.

A Small Thing

How that time in the hospital,
age 20 months and sitting
like a trained ballerina, knee bent,
thigh turned out flat on the crib mattress,
a tube in her nose, IV in the small arm,
the remnants of sobbing shaking her chest—
how when we showed her the new bib
we'd brought for her, she chuckled
heh-heh-heh and waited, smiling
while we tied it on around her neck.

If she could explain what pleased her so
and so easily, in the midst of misery—
was it the color (lilac),
the small floating clown figures,
an object she could recognize
with a familiar purpose
among so many unfamiliars—
if we could understand what tickled her then
we would start now to search, knowing
there are next times.

Sky Watch

No, she'd never seen a rainbow.
We watched the drizzly sky crack open
above the small suburban houses—
scant bits of blue, edges of light.
I wanted to show her one like the one
I'd seen from my fifth floor city window,
the schoolyard across newly abandoned
by ballplayers running from rain.

Not some pale wavering fragment,
but the complete arc, a band of color
distinct against vast grayness,
it rose from behind the white penthouse,
climbed into open sky above
water tanks and satellite dishes,
fell symmetrically toward
the low brownstones. Suspended
for minutes—the rainbow and I.
I wanted to shout through the glass
Look up! Look up!
to people in the street below
hurrying, heads down
beneath umbrellas.

Now as I watched with her,
my four-year-old grandchild,
there was just empty sky
and I wondered how she would bear
yet again not seeing one.
But she wandered off
cheerfully, to string beads.

Remnants of Sound

It started out like other hikes we'd taken up that path:
legs bending, then stretching to meet the steeply sloping earth.
Earth pockmarked with rocks or soft with moss.
We passed the cascades of whooshing foaming rush,
soon losing it all to quiet. And then aware—the air—
faintly tainted in high-pitched sound that gathered,
streamed, did not relent, shrieked, pierced
its way forward. Surrounded, enveloped in sound.
We pressed into it, through until it faded, died.
The same path back provoked the same crescendo.
Days later the news of local locust swarms.
When we went back, their broken shell-like skins
were everywhere—silent remnants,
an invisible force made visible,
the ghostly graveyard of an army that had disappeared.

Cochise Stronghold
Dragoon Mountains

He held out where I hike—
vigilant from granite cliffs,
hiding among boulders,
crags and spires, manzanita,
juniper, Arizona oak.

Apache, of the Chiracahua band,
a chief and leading warrior.
In this remote, rugged place
now named for him, Cochise
evaded and tormented his tormentors.

The landscape must have fed
not just his body. Pale rocks
that spear an azure sky, streambeds
flanked by ghostly sycamores,
the sound of saying *manzanita, man za ni ta.*

The trail winds gently higher,
the view ahead grows limited
to hill and sky and saddle's edge.
Cochise is buried here—
no living soul knows where.

Tree leaves whooshing in the wind,
birdspeak floating from behind
while I descend, as if, before I leave,
Cochise were signaling his secrets
and I could make them out.

We Took the Red-Eye

Midnight at the departure gate was lively
although the airport itself was still.
We were a bustling island in a sea
of dim deserted halls and shuttered snack bars.
Young mothers fed each other steady chatter,
sat crosslegged on the carpet laughing
while half-watched toddlers wandered.

The plane was late beyond
its scheduled lateness.

Off by herself quite unconcerned,
tall, slender, and barefoot,
a woman stretched out on the floor
sitting up to touch her toes,
her rhythm a metronome
keeping time in this place
of lost time and faltering rhythm.

Finally, like aging wine whose dregs
accumulate, our group was siphoned
into the plane. Then darkness was decreed
by personnel. A still, uneasy curtain fell
as bodies folded, leaned, slumped their way
into a mangled land of wakefulness or sleep.

Hours later in a different time zone
we were disgorged, dispersed
and left to stumble
through well-lit corridors, dodging
the purposeful who hurtled past us
in the opposite direction.
But this was home.

Disaster in October

A confluence of wind and wet snow
stormed through the city. Trees
still ripe with leaves and poised
to show their best Fall colors
held the unexpected weight
until they fell. Fragile branches
gave way. In Central Park
a thousand trees destroyed,
sprawled akimbo at the edges
of Fifth Avenue's stately sidewalks,
and lying unkempt as tangled hair
on hills and ancient bedrock.
No one was ready
bemoaned the Parks official,
as if he should have sent out
troops with brooms
to brush the snow off as it fell
and warned us,
Be prepared to mourn.

Men at the Construction Site

Directly across the narrow street
through our closed windows
we see them, each straddling
a rust-colored beam,
as if each beam were a wooden horse
and they riding with nothing to fear.

One day floors appear—
plates of corrugated silvery metal.

Now we see men scattered
floor to floor, visible all at once
in layers. Less empty space,
we have the illusion
they are moored and safe.

Arrayed singly or in groups
each works his role: lifts the pipe,
rivets, drills, reads specifications.

Slowly, they will be lost from view,
enclosed. We will strain to see
through two sets of windows,
the structure hiding its immense
complexity, the men performing
with no audience. Finally

they will disperse, the building set
to absorb those it was meant for.
But the men will have something
they can point to.

Consolation in Winter

Eagles have been spotted in the city
sailing ice floes south to the harbor,
catching fish along the way.
You go to look. Ice
reaching rough and still into the Hudson—
a tame Antarctica spawned from the shore.
Flowing, a central strip of white, empty.
Frozen layers at the edge are pierced
by coated ruins of former piers.

These frigid offerings—
eagles are not necessary here.

A Wider World

I was homesick for our cat—
how I would pick him up
by the scruff of the neck,
fling him, like a sack of potatoes
onto my shoulder so he could
drape himself there, blinking,
tolerant, until he wanted off.
I was in sleepaway camp,
an only child luxuriating
in constant companionship,
away from dread polio,
finding things I was good at
like racing fast and high jumps.
I lost my baby ways there—the night
a girl in my group called out
*It sounds like someone
is sucking their thumb!*
The darkness hid my shame.
I never sucked my thumb again.

At rest period, from my cot,
I looked out the open window
at a lawn rolling toward far hills
and longed for the cat. Later
I realized it was not about the cat
but about the space at home
my absence left for my parents,
who no longer loved each other.

Fraught History

Mother could not abide her own mother,
whom we visited only once,
driving for days. Years later
I still see Grandmother's hairy chin,
feel how repelled I was.
That trip was the last trip
my parents took together,
a failed effort at family
before they divorced. Along the way
we stopped at Niagara Falls—
as if the tumultuous roar
could drown out all the unspoken hostility
I sensed with my body, which was
carsick for the first and only time.

On the way home we detoured
to view the famous Mississippi.
It was lesser and browner than my imaginings.
I never saw Grandmother again.
What I heard of her was filtered
through my mother's bile.
Still, the old woman
helped raise my three cousins
after their mother—her other daughter—
fled from life down an elevator shaft
while they all lived in China, in the 40's.

In a carton are letters from China
and in my jewelry box,
a silver bracelet etched with dragons.

Camp Counselors Make Out

It was the summer of heat and
not just the weather—
we ran through boyfriends
by the week, trading them
like playing cards, music
we danced to pulsing our days.
I was dreamy and dazed,
a sleepy cat in the sun
led by the sure warm body of
the Negro swim counselor. This
was 50 years ago. We danced
on danger's edge, silently avoided
what wanted to happen.

One day, late in the season
I found my blond friend Sally
cuddled on a narrow cot
with another girl. *Lesbian*
was not a word we knew but
I could feel their heat and
feel my fear. Home again
I mooned for my black
dance partner, tried to imagine
his life, fretted over Sally –
the girlfriends and boyfriends
she betrayed. Cooler weather
was on its way.

The Lure

Wisteria, if you felt
your own dwindling,
could imagine the bare vine,
would you plunge more recklessly
from up to down the brownstone wall,
pour more hanging clusters
to play against the muddy stucco?
Would you perform your color
more deeply, or paler?
Yes the color, epitome
of lilac- violet- blue
How it lures me even when
you are nothing
but a charcoal vine.

After Chemotherapy

We pull it off like lovers who
manage to hide the truth
from their respective spouses,
ignore seismic signals
warnings of aftershocks
or the next big one—
pretend we don't live there.
True, the house sustained damage,
collapsed stairs and a large crack
in the living room wall
but restoration was skillful.
Only the third stair groaning softly
when the wind shifts
or when we pad up and down in the night,
escaping from dreams.

Not a Concert

About to leave
the Cancer Center lobby
live music washes over you,
cello and violin—chamber music
in this chamber where
an anxious hum of waiting
now flows beneath
the resonating strings.
Complex chords
you struggle to identify.

Your condition is stable
but instead of hustling home
you sit to listen
like a concertgoer
only there is no program,
no names to honor
the young musicians
who play so earnestly and
are mostly ignored
by women wearing turbans,
men bent over canes,
and their livelier companions.

Amid a blur of people swimming by
to higher floors and annual routine
you strain to focus on
the violin's excited song,
the cello's undertone
but no, impossible to grasp the music
or the lives of turbaned women
and bald men holding canes.

Stunning Blows

The mouse and I approached the steps
from opposite directions. Incongruous
against the smooth white marble,
its small gray body, solitary
and seemingly programmed
to march forward. When I yelped,
our doorman came bounding,
grabbed a "caution, wet floor" stand
and whacked the mouse
as if playing a game of cricket.
He's dead, declared the doorman
but I wasn't sure. Perhaps that mouse
was simply stunned at its rough treatment.

Stunned, like my friends—
the husband, plagued by
insomnia, turned out to be harboring
a raging liver cancer. Stunned
that the doctor told him by telephone
he has just weeks left to live.

I didn't linger
to contemplate the mouse
or check its status. When I returned
there were no signs
of its existence or demise.
But I still see it, like death,
moving toward me.

Second Wind
For Gerhard

The surgeons tuned you,
bypassed the years,
gave extra mileage.
Why should you not
stride off again,
climb mountains
mute in mist, emerge
to extravagant sunshine?
Once more the wind,
the weight of your pack,
limbs, sweat, breath.

Then, you will rest.

Alice Neel Paints a Portrait

of herself at 75, nude, working it
for five more years while breasts
sag lower, belly grows more lax,
body following its own path.
She is seated with weapons—
paint brush and rag. Look
at her watching you, the wall
in blue pastel, blue shadow
on leg and face, her old woman's
whiteness, the eyeglasses
for relentless vision. Look
at Alice seeing herself, knowing
what you will see.

Forget That

Forget that you forgot
your former student's name today
Forget you didn't recognize her face
until she said her name and
named the class she took with you
Forget that yesterday
you told a different student
you knew her mentor years ago
thinking that the mentor
was the student
whose face you didn't recognize
whose name you didn't know
Forget that yesterday
you made a special point
to ask that student to remember you
to her mentor-your-presumptive-former-student
whom you almost certainly
have never met and do not know
Forget that someday
you won't remind yourself
to forget

Flying

Such delight
on that small face
being lifted to shoulders.
What pleasure,
like dreams of flying,
the release
improbably real.

Is that why
we admire their flight—
those pelicans
sailing a cushion of air?
My dream-flights
were tree-level.
It was enough
then, would suffice
now when
I'm earth-bound,
no longer light enough
to be lifted.

The Key to Gramercy Park

No matter that the park is private
and I can't go in—I claim it.
I walk the park perimeter.
The park is mine to monitor.

Last week red tulips—luminescent—
hailed all who looked. Now
stubs and stems remain.
The corner where I stopped each day,
imbibing pink dogwood
and the pink-white tulips
shaped like roses that it hovered above
are flowering no longer. But further
is orange azalea, its flowers pale,
full, the branches spread apart
and taller than the standard white and red
nearby that wear their blooms
tight and densely packed.
Cherry, forsythia, magnolia, redbud
have passed into leaf. Still, a singular tree
I can't name drapes its pastel peach flowers
over the fence like a wedding canopy.

These gifts and losses, every year, mine.

About the Author

Felice Aull was born in Vienna and immigrated to the US with her parents. She holds a PhD in basic medical sciences and a more recent MA in humanities and social thought. While a full-time faculty member at New York University School of Medicine, she founded a widely used online resource, The Literature, Arts, and Medicine Database (http://litmed.med.nyu.edu/). She is now adjunct in the Division of Medical Humanities in NYU's Department of Medicine and spends much of her time writing, reading, and critiquing poetry. Her poetry has appeared in *Poet Lore, Margie, Ekphrasis, Third Wednesday, Umbrella, The Write Place At the Write Time, The Healing Muse, The Mom Egg,* and elsewhere. A finalist for the *Margie* 2007 Editor's Prize Best Poem, she has a poem in the anthology, *Letters to the World* (Red Hen Press, 2008). Her scholarly articles are published in *The Journal of Medical Humanities, Narrative,* and in other professional journals. She serves as associate editor of the journal, *Literature and Medicine* and is on the editorial board of *The Bellevue Literary Review*. She and her husband live in New York City. This is her first poetry collection.

Made in the USA
Columbia, SC
18 February 2020